AF125014

The Revolution of the MONEY-system
for the Benefit of all HUMANITY

The Revolution
of the MONEY-system
for the Benefit of all HUMANITY

_____

Rafael D. Kasischke

Bibliographical Information of the Deutsche Nationalbibliothek
This publication is listed in the Deutsche Nationalbibliographie of the
Deutsche Nationalbibliothek; detailed bibliographical information can
be accessed under http: //dnb.d-nb.de

© 2014 Rafael D. Kasischke

Printing, Production and Layout:
BoD – Books on Demand, Norderstedt

ISBN: 978-3-7357-7149-0

This book is dedicated to my children,
Melina and Delano, and their future children.
Melina and Delano are representatives
of their generation, just as their future children
will be for the following generation.

May these generations gain a new consciousness
about the world, their mission in life and the purpose
and tasks of fellow human beings.

And may the children of the future be born
with the awareness that LOVE and the HEART
are the most important preconditions for humanity.

Half of the Book Prize will be contributed as a donation
in the **"FUND for the next Generation"**.

Contents

Prologue 9

Introduction 11

Our MONEY awareness until today 16

The association of MONEY
with higher Principles 21

The Purpose of MONEY 29

The Use of MONEY 33

Our new appreciation of MONEY 40

The Power of MONEY 43

Our inner Wealth 46

The next Generation 50

Would you like to pass something on –
by which you are remembered? 54

FUND for the next Generation 57

My own Experiences 59

Prologue

Today we live in a world of great change. The most important and earth-shattering change will be experienced in relation to our ATTITUDE to the material.

Many people have placed their security in their materialism.

My heartfelt wish is to support these people in their interior lives, to free them from anxiety and depression, to show them their innate potential, and to provide a new approach towards the material. For it is not the material which represents security for people, but our own gifts, **talents and potential** that make up the strength of a person; and thus **his or her security.**

I want to show people how they can partake in the NEW, and how they can emerge stronger from this upheaval – both in the financial as well as in the emotional sphere.

This change means a **new beginning in our ATTITUDE** to many things.

VALUES are changing now. More and more people are withdrawing their attention and appreciation from the economic system because they see through its faults and injustices.

At the same time, we are beginning to realize how we really want to live, and what makes us happy.

We should open our HEARTS. And we should free our minds, so that we are capable of utterly new thoughts.

However, many people still think in terms of old models and structures.
They have not yet realized that the world is in transition, and that the old structures are no longer valid. There are some considerably new, invisible processes underway.

People who are open to change, experience personal upheavals and difficult times: existential fears etc. The ground is pulled from under them in the truest sense. But they will emerge strengthened from this situation, provided that they remain open to personal change and not fall back into the old system.

Everything that happens serves for purification and renewal. Our potentials are thereby revealed. We separate ourselves from much, and decide for our true self instead of for our ego. Thus, we open ourselves to our authentic being and to unconditional LOVE.

Responsibility, VALUES and spirituality shape the new paradigm.
They bear witness to the new era of sustainable economy. If a system is in crisis, the opportunity emerges of something maturing, opening up and changing inwardly. A crisis is good because a new quality can grow in business. A crisis is healthy. It cleanses – and it creates something new.
The old tree gets sick and decays so a new one can grow.

"Change occurs when there is a confluence of both changing values and economic necessity, not before."
John Naisbitt

Introduction

"We have a dream": We would like people to be happy, content and healthy – emotionally as well as financially. And we want to create WEALTH – for as many people as possible.
Therefore, we need a new ATTITUDE towards money:

A meaningful, respectful and loving approach to MONEY.

This pertains to a new VALUE system.
And it includes a BALANCE between material and immaterial affairs.

We are experiencing a tumultuous, and at the same time, valuable upheaval in world history: This change takes place in **society**, our **mentality** and most especially **in how we deal with MONEY**. For it is not only the world that is transforming, but **MONEY** as well.

MONEY has always been a MAGNET for humanity.
Many people have followed this MAGNET.
And so, MONEY obtained a monumental status.
Many have worshipped it as a "golden calf". For them, the pursuit and accumulation of money became the aim of their existence because they believed that money would make them happy.
HEALTH, and life itself, played a secondary role.
However, did we all become happier because of this?

Now the time has come to **change our attitudes to-wards MONEY, together with our beliefs and under-standing of it**. Thus the world of money transforms into a world of MONEY & SPIRIT.

> **Money should serve people –**
> **people shouldn't serve money.**

In the future, money will be connected with the HEART. But first, we have to **HEAL THE SOURCE**: that is to say, the way in which people have accumulated their money in the past.

Thus, we will contribute to the healing of our SOULS because many people have – like Goethe's Faust – "sold their souls to Mephistopheles".

Through money, human beings have been tempted by greed, EGO and power.

What matters now is that people rediscover their SOULS and become aware of their true purpose; that they learn to live their truth and heal their past, before going "home".

And it's about HEALING with respect to society and reconstituting all the related resources that we have taken advantage of: the soil, water, nature, labour ... and so much more!

Now it is time to give back what we have taken, and to invest again in these resources.

And we should PASS SOMETHING ON.
When I was a child, my mother asked me:
"What would you like to be one day?"
When I did not have an answer to that, she said:

"You should build something that you can be proud of in your life, so that you leave something to the world, something that is remembered."

I want to PASS SOMETHING ON to my children and the entire younger generation, because in the end, that's what's important to us as human beings: our CHILDREN and GRANDCHILDREN.

At the same time, I would like to give something to our younger and older generation: the message that our inner wealth is far greater, more valuable and richer than our external assets. And that we should not fixate on material things, but rather on this inner wealth.
We need to preserve this knowledge, and rely upon it.

Therewith, I want to demonstrate that there is something more than just the material world, something greater and far more profound, something that we all carry within ourselves because we are born with it: our **talents and potential**.

This is what matters now: not to rely on mere exteriors, but on yourself – on your inner strengths; because material values are transient and only last a single lifetime.
We should deal with our inner values in a dignified and benign manner.
We humans are trustees and custodians of the treasures which were placed into our cradle at birth, and that we will leave when we pass on.
All we can take with us are our impressions of how we have dealt with these treasures.

However, how do we as human beings actually deal with these treasures?

Do we utilize our monies wisely? And are we dealing with MONEY correctly, at all?

Also, how can it be that in spite of material prosperity, many people look for a MEANING – a meaning to life and happiness?

The answer is: **We must reconcile MONEY with MEANING**. That is because, until now, there has been no connection between them. But how can we acquire MEANING? And how much does it cost? We know that MEANING is not something we can simply purchase. The only way to gain MEANING, is by using our SPIRIT.

And we need to connect this SPIRIT with MONEY.

We have to bring SPIRIT into MONEY.

We have to realize that **MONEY cannot make us happy.** This requires a change in our INTENTION. It's no longer about earning MONEY all for oneself in life or raising "a golden calf", so that we can satisfy our EGOS.

In order to be happy and healthy as people, **we must look on MONEY differently** – we must learn a new AWARENESS.

Our INTENTION can and should be to do something GOOD with MONEY: to use it for HUMANKIND and their needs, for their EDUCATION, HEALTH, NUTRITION, and for the implementation of their ideas and talents.

If we change our INTENTION and – having growth as our goal – do something good for ourselves **AND for others**, then we will be rewarded, and we will get something back.

If we combine our MONEY with inner VALUES and our HEARTS, and use it for mankind, we achieve CONTENT-MENT AND HEALTH. And, in addition, our investment GROWS.

In the future, MONEY will make people happy, because they will no longer look upon it with FEAR, POWER, GREED or EGO, but connect their HEARTS with it, and make it available with JOY.

Our MONEY awareness until today

> *"Money is an inestimably important instrument,*
> *a means that can be good and*
> *valuable to possess and use,*
> *but that can lead into bondage,*
> *if we let it possess us."*
>
> Snah Sneleiw

The world is going through a fundamental transformation – MONEY too is subject to this great change. However, an even more significant and world-shaking change is happening to our ATTITUDE, i.e. our mentality towards the material world.

That is because, until now, many people have been aligned with the material world.

This change is good and necessary, because the river – the MONEY FLOW – has been contaminated by the overvaluation of material thinking.

No values swim in this river, rather too much falsehood and dishonesty along with corruption, embezzlement, greed for profit and more money, egotism and social indifference. Many people no longer feel happy, they do not see any MEANING any more, and have no joy in life. We have to clean out this river.

For when the river water is clean, the people are satisfied. What cleanse the river are truth and honesty, transparency and justice, trust and faith, decency and ethics, prudence and humility, as well as the inclusion of public spirit and common welfare.

The new MONEY FLOW arises within us, and leads from the inside to the outside.
It is based on a new ATTITUDE, and a new FAITH – on a new relationship with money.

We're talking about a TRANSFORMATION of MONEY:
- away from the purely material and towards a UNITY between spirit and the material
- away from the previous focus on the external, and towards the realization that money has an inner side.

Because MONEY influences our inner life – our THOUGHTS and FEELINGS. Fears, depression and other emotions are closely connected with MONEY.
In order to get out of this "vicious circle", we must develop a new AWARENESS and RELATIONSHIP towards money.

So we have to re-think things. We cannot look on money as before, i.e. as a separate product, and see something material that is separate from us.
MONEY is not separate from us. MONEY is closely connected to every human being.
This is a new and important insight: MONEY is connected to our higher self or SOUL.
They relate to each other in a symbiotic relationship.

Before, we considered MONEY to be abstract from us; as personal property.

Many people deal with money in a selfish and obstinate manner. They hold onto material things and make themselves dependent on it.

This results in FEAR regarding their money and material things.

But money is not separate from us as human beings. MONEY has a relationship with each of us. It is linked to each one of us, and has a story to tell.

And there is a reason why some people have lots of money, and others have less.

I have accompanied many entrepreneurs in my life. One thing has caught my attention time and again: that as long as these people work with their own money, they are happy – even if they are experiencing losses. Why? Because these losses result from their own decisions.

But when they place their money in the hands of outsiders, like banks or money managers for example, they actually become disconnected from their money. What does this mean? Money is connected to us as individuals – to our hearts.

When we part with it, we separate our money from our hearts. We divide our ENERGY relationship with our money.

In order to reinforce this energy, it is important in future to build up a feeling – a sense of enthusiasm, a bond – with our MONEY, and to give our money a noble purpose.

I asked a well-known author who wrote a book about selling with "Noble Purpose" the question: "How would MONEY change if it had a noble purpose? Would the money then grow successfully?"

His answer was clear: "Yes!" He himself had experience with prior investments in company shares.

He had a heartfelt attachment to these companies, knowing them personally, and knew that these companies had a "noble purpose" at their foundation.

Therefore, the companies had inspired his heart and feelings. So he was connected to these companies. And he had taken full responsibility for his money. With both investments he had great success.

With subsequent investments, he experienced no such success as he did not feel connected to them and had given his money over to be managed, therefore not having been able to give his money a "noble purpose".

This author pointed out yet another important factor to me: that we should actually physically hold MONEY in our hand, so that we can build a connection to it.

In other words, we should accept and spend money in cash and not pay using credit cards.

Even if we study portfolio statements: these are only numbers on a computer.

We cannot establish a personal, emotional connection with these virtual (fictitious) figures.

The message: INNER VALUES are the prerequisites for EXTERNAL VALUES

And our SPIRIT and faith in something higher than this earthly existence also belong to these inner values.

Spirituality will play an important role in the future. When we are in touch with our inner values, we can accept external wealth as a gift; we can enjoy it, and pass it on meaningfully. The condition needed in order to connect with our inner values is the awareness that everything is interconnected.

Future researcher Patricia Aburdene has identified **spirituality** as the megatrend of our age. Old-school capitalism has had its day, she says. We are turning our view to the significant new beginning of a conscious capitalism.
We humans have the power to transform capitalism: as investors, consumers and managers.
And capitalism has the power to change the world.

The association of MONEY with higher Principles

"In the beginning was the silence.
The silence of the rocks, the sky, the grasses.
The silence of the night, and the morning of creation.
Long before anything was mentioned by name,
before mountain became mountain,
stone became stone, earth became earth,
there was creative silence.
Eternity of all ideas and words,
Respect for the mystery of life.
Before I, before we all,
were called by name,
the world was without a word. "
Native American Wisdom – by Wolfgang Peoplau

Everything is ENERGY: our thoughts, our emotions, our bodies – and our MONEY.
Energy must flow. When it flows, the energy comes back to us.
If we are too engrossed in the mind, energy cannot flow because it is not connected to our hearts.
It is the same with money. When we are too concerned with the accumulation of MONEY without employing our hearts, it can neither flow nor grow.
MONEY will only grow if we combine it with GOOD INTENTIONS, and a NOBLE PURPOSE.
If treated negatively or indifferently, it will not flourish.

We will not afford materialism the same importance as before, and instead we will make new room for spirituality. Along the way, our faith in ourselves will help us, and connected with that, our faith in something greater, higher and universal.

I wonder if a spiritual, universal world exists. In my opinion and, according to my personal experiences, the spirit world plays a significant role, a far greater role than the material world – that which we cannot perceive in the immaterial world is more powerful than anything we do see.

> *"Blessed are those who have not seen and yet believe."*
> Jesus

So the solution to today's financial crisis, and to our life and identity crisis, lies within us: **in our thinking, our thoughts and intentions**, and not in externals.
The solution is not to change external circumstances, but rather, the transformation must start within us as humans. Only then will the external be reformed.
This means that **we should change our inner attitude, i.e. our thinking patterns and beliefs**. Our inner attitude should be directed towards more satisfaction, more gratitude and more optimism.

It is about recognizing that money is not everything in life. In any case, it does not provide security, because at some point we have to let it go.

True security lies within us, only from this does true RECOGNITION and REPUTATION arise.

So we should not try to achieve SECURITY or recognition and reputation, through external values. What happens when nothing remains of material wealth? Our worries and fears grow.

To prevent this, we need to expand our inner status.

We have to become aware of our **inner VALUES,** and give less importance to our **external VALUES,** so that we achieve a **BALANCE**.

We must become aware that material belongs to SPIRIT. The material and the spiritual are interconnected.

We have to learn and understand that we can create that which is material, with SPIRIT. Because SPIRIT is the premise for making something TANGIBLE.

There is no matter without spirit – without consciousness. Science teaches us this.

Our consciousness creates reality, and as such, they are not separated.

Before something is materialized, we first develop IDEAS and THOUGHTS. A certain spirit underlies these thoughts and ideas, upon which they can thrive.

We first envisage what we want to create on the material level.

The crucial point here is **our mental INTENTION**.

The INTENTION should be positive, and come from the HEART. That is the key to success.

> *"People should learn to think with the heart,*
> *and feel with the mind."*
> Theodor Fontane

So far the INTENTION of people has been to accumulate MONEY, and to multiply it.

However, this intention is no longer appropriate because it does not bring happiness.

In the future, it will no longer be a question of multiplying money and possessions.

In the future, people will earn MONEY by bringing benefits to themselves AND to society, and it will all come from the heart.

Our lesson:

Our INTENTION is – and our intention is connected to the HEART – to serve people and the environment with our commitment to money. This investment will then multiply, and the MONEY FLOW will flourish.

We simply have to connect MONEY with HEART.
MONEY is the result of a product or service produced by us.

The HEART is associated with this product or service, but not always with the resulting outcome: MONEY.

Till now, we have handed this money over to institutions such as banks, insurance companies, investment funds, etc. We thus relinquished ourselves of the responsibility for our MONEY, instead of taking care of it ourselves, and taking personal responsibility.

In previous decades, the financial industry responsibly invested their client's MONEY, so it could flow. The flow of money was interrupted, because institutions and governments ceased to take care of their clients' and citizens' money in an honorable way, and their INTENTION instead focused on the maximization of profits and return – in a partially unethical manner.

If we learn how to properly deal with MONEY from the HEART, then we do it FOR THE BENEFIT OF ALL, and not for the BENEFIT of the individual, or the EGO.

Therefore the message is:
MONEY must serve the BENEFIT OF ALL.

"It would be better
for the people and the world,
if money would have a heart,
and heart more money."
Jewish proverb

The function of MONEY is not to serve and satisfy the EGO, but rather to serve our SOUL.
Out of the SOUL emanates happiness, health, harmony and joy.
The EGO, on the other hand, creates greed and fear, envy and resentment, discontent and disease.
We need to learn to reflect on how to use our money for **the benefit of all**, which will lead to the healing of our SOULS and consciences.

Human souls could be healed, if their money were transformed.

There are many FUNDS, which have not been generated ethically.

It's not just money from the present generation, but also from earlier ones.

For example, if entrepreneurs have made their money from the production of war materials or other goods, whereby man or the environment has come to harm, this is MONEY which is not ethical in origin.

This could have an impact on the health of future generations. Anything from financial problems or health problems to depression and suicide can be the result.

A correlation between such funds and mental or emotional diseases has not been realized academically – to the best of my knowledge. But I am deeply convinced that there is a correlation between such monies and mental diseases.

> *"Money is our mirror.*
> *It can do more than*
> *reflect only our shadows.*
> *It is a mirror of our soul."*
> *Unknown author*

I have met many people in my life, and was always interested in their life stories.

One day, I learnt of the following family history:

A successful businessman lived a happy life, filled with material wealth.

One day his good luck ran out. He was dismissed from his job. He looked for a new one, but times were difficult. So he started his own business.

However, even these efforts were not very successful and he therefore continued to worry about his young family. His wife had supported him until then, but soon began to feel that it really wasn't working anymore.

She too was worried. An energy blockage developed between man and wife.

The businessman felt that there were not only blockages between him and his wife, but also between him and MONEY. He set out to search for the causes, and discovered the following:

His great grandparents had been business people and had two drug stores before the Second World War. They sold various chemicals, among other things.

These chemicals were used for various purposes.

Although it is not proven, my interlocutor thinks that these chemicals were also used to poison Jews during the Holocaust.

The daughter of the great grandparents, however, was very close to the Jewish community and helped some of them escape Germany. This daughter gave birth to a daughter during the Second World War.

After the Second World War the mother committed suicide. The official reason: she suffered from depression. The daughter in turn gave birth to four children after the war. One of the children also suffered from depression and later also committed suicide. Other family members also suffered from anxiety of one kind or another.

How can we explain the relationship to MONEY here? The originally earned money was not "clean" because it was probably not generated merely from the sale of chemicals or pharmaceuticals.

My interlocutor concluded that he had to heal the situation. He also changed his attitude towards Money. So the blockages were removed. And the money began to flow again.

The aim is therefore to transform the original INTENTION of the generated money into a GOOD INTENTION, and thus to turn "bad money" into GOOD MONEY.

We transform MONEY, by using it to meet people's needs, such as in EDUCATION, HEALTH, organic agriculture, clean drinking water, the fostering and financing of young people and therefore entrepreneurship.

The Purpose of MONEY

"Money and wealth are not bad,
only people can use them
for good or bad."
Stoic Philosophical View

Our current MONEY is neither well allocated, nor well distributed.
It is in the hands of a few people, and a few financial institutions of the world.
A wider distribution of money would mean an economic boom for everyone involved. However, a requirement for this is a new awareness with regard to dealing with money.

HOW do we use money?
MONEY should set things in MOTION, which lead to inner and outer wealth.
MONEY should therefore create BENEFIT, bring ADDED VALUE, i.e. flourish.
Therefore it has to be used where it can grow.
In order for money to grow, it needs assistance – i.e. spiritual support.

It's not just the question of **WHAT we invest our MONEY in**.
But it's also about **HOW we use MONEY**, and how we DEAL with it.

We need to connect positive THOUGHTS and INTENTIONS to money and use it positively. Then investments will grow.

When we plant the SEED with good INTENTIONS and THOUGHTS, and positive HEART energy for the benefit of all, **then we receive a positive crop. This is the key to long term and gratifying success.**

WHERE do we allocate the money so it brings BENEFIT and ADDED VALUE?

We know that money is ENERGY. So it's not a question of where the money will be "safely invested", but where this money ENERGY can bring maximum BENEFIT.

MONEY needs to be meaningfully allocated.

My credo: money deserves the creativity of people. And humans conceive new ideas. New products are created from these ideas, from which something new arises. We would not have artificial lighting or railways, nor cars or aircraft, if the ideas for these products had not been developed by humans.

We need to allocate money in a way that helps and serves mankind.

How can we accomplish this goal? It's only possible through a new form of capitalism: **the humanization of capital**. Because capital and people go hand in hand.

Humanization of money will occur as soon as we recognize that money is a medium with the purpose of serving mankind.

The Dalai Lama says:

"Wealth is not bad. It just depends on how we use it. There is nothing wrong with it, if it has been acquired honestly, and neither other people nor the environment has come to harm. But in so far as this is not so, our society suffers.

The gratification in the mind of many wealthy people, who do not share money, and just wish to accumulate it, leads to sickness. Rich people should instead help to reduce poverty. The selfish pursuit of only ever earning even more money, and accumulating more possessions, harms the individual, and his or her family.

Capitalism places great emphasis on wealth creation, and its distribution. But the wealth is not distributed. We see that the rich get richer, and the poor get poorer, and worse that people count for little. Prosperity is the prerequisite for a happy life."

**Money should serve people –
people shouldn't serve money.**

We should use MONEY for those things that we humans and the earth need, and which lead to new innovations that are useful, and meet our real needs.

However, more and more money is spent that does not correspond to the deep needs and beliefs of people. The reason: the globalized economy is still characterized by the old values of profit maximization, and the exploitation of people and nature.

This is not sustainable in the long run; on the contrary, it is destructive.

The financial economy of the future must use the power of money primarily for life-enhancing and life-sustaining goals. It must develop an attitude of appreciation for all life. And it must return to its function of service.

How can this shift and transformation of money be positive and succeed?
There is a control in place: the wisdom of the heart. **Using the wisdom of the heart, a fundamental transformation can come underway,** which means that the people who deal with the power of money face life. For the heart is the most important keeper of rhythm in the body.

> *"Of all the possessions on earth the most valuable is to have a heart."*
> Johann Wolfgang von Goethe

The Use of MONEY

*"Wealth is of no real value
unless it is used to serve the people."*
Sheikh Zayed bin Sultan Al Nahyan

We know that our real ASSETS lay in our **potential and talents, in our creativity, our ideas and our imagination**. With this wealth, we can always build something new.

We know that our OBSTACLES are our worries, doubts and fears, our clinging and dependance on material assets and our EGO.

We can overcome these obstacles, and build a new fundamental for our lives if we change our attitude:
Our INTENTION should be to use money in a meaningful way.
For this, we must open our hearts, and use our money for projects that appeal to our hearts. Then money will have a positive effect on our emotions.
So which projects touch our HEARTS?

a)   **Investments in EDUCATION**

We humans want to experience JOY.
We humans want to be HEALTHY.
EDUCATION is the foundation for humanity.
And in this we should invest.

Because without education we cannot be aware of our talents, our creativity and our health.

- We need LIFE and VALUE schools.

- We need TALENT, HEALTH and AGRICULTURAL schools.

- We need a new SCHOOL SYSTEM for our children – around the globe.
  Because our education and training systems are antiquated.
  They are based on traditional patterns of thinking.
  This is because our educational system educates only on the rational level.
  The other aspects of intelligence such as spiritual, intuitive, mental, emotional and creative intelligence are not encouraged, and therefore cannot be developed.
  But this is the issue: to develop these talents and potential and thus liberate enthusiasm and creativity.

  New concepts already exist. And more concepts are emerging.

- We need EDUCATION CENTERS, which offer a dual training system.

b) Investments in HEALTH

The second most important foundation for humanity is HEALTH.
Without health, we cannot fully realize our talents and creative force.
We must consume healthy food, live healthily and maintain a healthy mind.
For this, we need HEALTH schools and HEALTH centers.

The teaching of holistic healthcare includes the detoxification of the body, the use of healing remedies including alkaline water, learning about our body cells, healthy eating, healthy living, physical health, the teaching of emotional health, a healthy mind, and beliefs in any kind of spirituality as a substantial part of the well-being of people as well as the decent use of money.

c) Investments in PEOPLE and their potential

An equally important fundamental for mankind is the financing of business ideas, and thus the promotion of entrepreneurship.
Because MONEY is a means, an instrument for the promotion of life and living.
We should use money for necessities that we people and the planet need, and which lead to innovation.

We will invest money in VALUES which touch our HEARTS – for responsible, meaningful and sustainable projects.

We will support people in a way that will provide benefits to employees, customers and the environment. They will use their heart and mind, creativity and intuition.
That is the basis for economic success.

"Sustainability is the most succesful business model because it satisfies mankind forever and not only for a moment."
Dr. h.c. Helmut Maucher

Our credo: People will enjoy their work as soon as their true potentials have been discovered. Work is fun when it meets our vocations because it is then no longer "work", but a passion.

People will no longer just learn and practice a profession, but instead will follow their GIFTS, which may be many and varied. They will not consider these gifts to be a JOB that they have to do. Instead they will enjoy the FULFILLMENT of their duties.

When happy and satisfied people offer services and products, this has a positive impact on customers and therefore on the company.

One example is the Latin American coffee shop chain "Crepes & Waffles".
The company only employs single mothers. It gives them the opportunity to work under humane conditions, and to care for their children at the same time.
The company is like a second family for these mothers. It provides them with a social network:
good salaries, health insurance and child care in nursery school, tuition and school fees.
After a certain period of employment, the company offers home financing through an interest-free loan.
The result: the mothers work with great commitment and a sense of responsibility.
And the company makes money and is successful.

d) **Investments in the EARTH:**
   agriculture, water, energy

Private investors, foundations and institutional investors are interested in investing their funds MEANINGFULLY. In addition to education, health and investment in people, the use of money for other human needs such as food, water and energy is of immense importance.

What is our EARTH offering: the soil and the ocean.
- We should invest in the soil – in projects where the soil is highly appreciated and respected.
  People will treat the soil in a very special way.
  New procedures will be developed and patented.

It will look like this:

Investors acquire or lease farmland. This is first revitalized to obtain the best yields, and to make people healthy.

The new farmers will have previously been trained in our agricultural school.

We will teach them to handle the soil, seed and crop in a conscious way – that is to say – in a new, prosperous manner. So we will give these people a new awareness, and support them in their personal development.

This work corresponds to their passion and vocational calling.

The crop is sold. The profit is used according to the requests of the respective investors:

The foundations use them according to their foundation's purpose.

The pension funds use them to finance the pensions for retirees.

The private investor uses his profits for his personal needs, or contributes a part for the common good; for example, for the financing of value or life schools.

- And we should invest in WATER.
  Because water is the basis of all life.
  It is the nutrient for our soil.
  It drives turbines, and provides us humans with energy.
  The investment in WATER – especially in drinking water sources – is therefore of great importance.

- The same is true for ENERGY.
  New forms of energy will be developed. We need
  to invest in young companies that create these new
  forms of energy.

  The financing of agriculture, drinking water and
  new energy projects is of outstanding importance
  for the evolution of the Earth!

Our new appreciation of MONEY

"Be the change you want to see in the world."
Mahatma Gandhi

When we, as human beings, exemplify this new way of using money and spread knowledge about it among investors, inspiring them to use their money differently than before and make this money available to many people, a broader distribution of capital among people is created.

And a wider distribution of money means a macroeconomic boom for all involved.

In the future, money will not be soulless; instead we will use it with good intentions and from the heart, at the same time giving out positive energy through our soul. Good INTENTIONS, HEART and positive ENERGY are intangibles. If we add them to our investments, we gain inner satisfaction.

And therefore, we build up our inner wealth and make ourselves aware of it.

So we connect MONEY with higher principles and a higher knowledge: consciousness, mind power, heart energy.

We thus create for the next generation both – a material as well as an immaterial foundation. By immaterial foundation, I mean the recognition of a new attitude and perspective on material things; achieving inner satisfaction and well-being as well as the discovery of individual potential and talents.

We teach people, corporations and institutions a new awareness in dealing with money so that it can flow again, i.e. be used productively – for the benefit of people, businesses and their employees as well as society in general. The basis of our teachings are VALUES – inner values such as: truth and honesty, transparency, justice, respect for others and self-esteem, a sense of community, trust and faith, compassion and love.
And so we make a pure river from an impure one.

Mankind carries these VALUES within themselves from birth. But they have not been developed or are no longer in their consciousness. Inner wealth has received little attention until now. Instead, the CONSCIOUSNESS of many people has been focused on material assets, because we believed that this would make us HAPPY and allow us to gain RECOGNITION and a good REPUTATION.

Our task today is to reformulate the objectives of society. Ways of thinking must be changed – starting at school, and particularly at universities. Predominantly, the teaching of economics will be subject to a fundamental change, because a new movement has emerged: the **economics of happiness**. In the future, the well-being of society is what will be important. This is the new gross domestic product.

The business model of banks today is also being put to the test.

A new business model is emerging. We have to return to the actual task of banks: taking and giving, and thereby using our HEARTS and having good INTENTIONS.

The benefits to the lender will be multiple: better health, a clear conscience and inner satisfaction.

In addition, he will have a financial and social return through supporting other people in their personal development and discovery of new ideas.

The Power of **MONEY**

Some people wonder whether money is „MAGIC". Because some people attract money in a seemingly magical and playful way. Most however, do not.
Can we learn this "magic"? Can we learn how to "attract" money?
The answer is: Yes.

We can "attract" money if we change our ATTITUDE towards money, and develop a new CONSCIOUSNESS.

- We need to change our INTENTION:
  no longer placing the focus on MONEY and financial return, but on the well-being and health of all.

- We need to develop ENTHUSIASM – Enthusiasm for using our potential and working with it.
  Therewith, automatically attracting customers and therefore, money.
  Today many people lack enthusiasm, meaning of life, spiritual faith and trust. Therefore, they attract no money.
  We need to earn and to use MONEY with ENTHUSIASM.

- We need to invest in pursuits which touch our hearts.

- Some people have to learn not to detain money because in fear to loose it.

- Other people have to learn not to look on MONEY negatively or indifferently.
  They must learn to receive MONEY with joy and gratefulness.

A good example of monetary success and the "attraction" of money is **Warren Buffet.**
He is one of the richest people on earth.

His INTENTION is to earn money for others – not for himself only.
He has not used money to build a "golden calf".
He lets money flow: He takes it from investors, invests it and gives it back.
He therefore lets go of money and doesn't withhold it.
He does not look upon money with fear, power, greed and ego.
He has joy in his work and does this with enthusiasm.
"I LOVE my job", he says. Therefore, the money grows.
In fact, he has already donated much of his money.

One can therefore clearly see the ease of financial success through his example.
His investments have been successful in our monetary system till present, insofar as they have brought financial returns.

Other conditions for investment will be at the basis of the course of change.
That is to say, the focus will no longer be placed solely on the tangible return on investment.

The secret of MONEY thus lays within us humans: within our THOUGHTS and AWARENESS – our faith and perception – and in our INTENTIONS.
And this POWER OF THOUGHT is energy.

Our inner Wealth

*"The great challenge of the Modern Age
lies not in changing the world
but in changing ourselves.
Be the change you want to see
in the world."*
Mahatma Gandhi

We human beings possess **inner wealth**, and also to a certain extent, external wealth.
So far, we humans have tended to focus on outer wealth, but in the future inner wealth will gain significantly in importance; because inner wealth is more important than external wealth, which in itself is transitory. Inner wealth however, which is our soul, we retain forever. We take our inner wealth with us when we leave the earth.

Our task is to discover this inner wealth, and develop it. Because it is exactly this immaterial potential that makes up the – inner – strength of a person. We should empower other people, so that they can recognize their **true inner wealth** and thus their **inner GOLD**.
And this inner GOLD is connected to the SOUL.

The meaning of life is to learn, to gain experience and to give love.
The goal is to transform negative energies into positive ones, and to unite opposites.

The future goal is the UNITY or BALANCE between
the inside and the outside,
inner and external values,
the material and the spiritual,
the individual and society,
male and female energy.

I know many people: people with money, people without money, happy people and peoplewho are searching – for meaning, partnership, joy and happiness.

We can assist these people in their life journeys, give them VALUES, show understanding, be a role model and help them to become aware of their own life cycle in order to live a more contented life.
However, my insight and experience is that everyone must go their own way, because this corresponds to the themes of their lives and their life tasks.

> *"You cannot teach a man anything,*
> *you can only help him find it within himself."*
> *Galileo Galilei*

People are born with certain vocations and talents. Through experiences with the environment, the pressures of society or other influences, diversion switches are set up within them, which direct them towards certain professional and family structures, which are actually not conducive to true inner satisfaction and the execution of their soul plan. They therefore become unhappy with themselves, with their professional situation and possibly with their families, but also in material terms, such as when dealing with money or other material values. MONEY then becomes a replacement value, instead of bringing their potential and talents to the world and letting others share it.

It more often becomes a matter of amassing outer riches.

But we, as humans, all have the ability to change our lives and adapt our attitudes.

My credo: Man is a creative being. He creates his whole life: his wealth or poverty, his health or disease, his happiness or misfortune. However, very few people are aware of the POWER of their THOUGHTS, FEELINGS and BELIEFS, because the majority have been left in ignorance.

> *"The more experience I gather, the more I realize that man himself is the cause of his happiness as well as his misery."*
> *Mahatma Gandhi*

What does **inner wealth** mean? It is our potentials and talents, in other words, the gifts and vocations with which every human being is born. From these, **creativity and inspiration** grow. And **ideas** are developed out of creativity and inspiration. **New developments and inventions** arise from those ideas that are of great importance, both for humanity and the personal evolution of the creator.

With these developments and inventions, we create something **innovative**.
And therefore regain MEANING and JOY – joy for life.

We must learn how to find our inner wealth and live it.
When we understand and implement this, we will be happy.
Because happiness arises from:
1.   Knowledge and awareness of our inner dimension – our inner wealth and our positive and negative sides,
2.   Acceptance, i.e. by accepting our inner dimension.
But accepting it and living it proves difficult for many.

The next Generation

We should give very special attention to the next generation.
Because our children are our future.
Today's youth come to the world with so much potential and talents, and equipped with great gifts.
In fact I would even claim: They are better than or, at least, different from previous generations. For among young people, quite a new way of thinking – a creative and constructive way – is recognizable.
They possess much of what is needed to make our earth a better place. Many of them have gained this potential along the way. These gifts need only be recognized and developed.

The positive here, is that we are now in a position to make these talents visible – or conscious – to do what was not possible in previous generations. For the youth of today have a particular task: they must take over the rudder that steers our planet, and do this in a more humane, ethical and morally conscious way than previous generations.

Decency, honesty, truth, helpfulness and solidarity are already cornerstones of their common lives.

They seek cooperation and not competition. And they will earn recognition and respect due to their contribution to the common good.

I look at the new generation as having a prosperous condition and future.

They have – without either their or their parents' knowledge – a world before them whose inhabitants will no longer search for **happiness and meaning**, but will actually live it because they have **common ideals and values**; because the importance of money and material things will take on a lower value, and inner wealth will play a greater role.

However one handicap for our young people exists in the form of our education and training systems. This stems from old patterns of thinking. In these systems of education, only the rational level is formed. Other potentials and intelligences are not fostered and therefore not brought to fulfillment. But this is exactly what is important: to develop these talents and potentials, thereby unleashing creativity.

We will work to bring new ways of thinking to the fore in order to activate and develop the five intelligences – the spiritual, the intuitive, the mental, the emotional and creative, so that young people can use them in the future.

So far four fifths of these intelligences have not been cultivated in the economy due to one-sided education and training. Therefore inspiration, meaning, fascination and passionate enthusiasm could not be realized. This is paralyzing the businesses of today.

Today it's more important than ever to integrate all these intelligences. The integration and use of this entire intelligence potential is the basis for leading a company into economic success in a humane and socially healthy manner.

So we have to pay attention to the next generation, so that the seed can sprout and significant results be attained.
Young people must be encouraged – both in their talents and business ideas.

And we don't just need to make proper education and training available to young people, but also give them the opportunity to put their ideas into action. When the older generation makes MONEY "unconditionally" available to them, it becomes possible for them to realize their potential.
After all, MONEY remains on earth. We cannot take it with us when we leave. It is therefore part of the money cycle to transfer this medium from the older to the younger generation – with the advice to deal wisely with it.

Wise and experienced counselors will guide the older and the younger generation They must accompany this process of investments, and evaluate young people: Their gifts and potentials, their ethical and moral faculties, as well as their business concepts.

The message here is: The transfer from the older generation to the younger one.

Currently, the older generation still holds firmly to the material world. They just cannot let go. Their focus is still on material return. But in their HEARTS, it is about their CHILDREN and GRANDCHILDREN.

We strive to convince older people to pass something onto the younger generation through which posterity will remember them, something that makes a difference in society.

In that way, they will not only make their children and grandchildren happy, but also themselves. Through such use of money, they will get an emotional return.
The investor can experience the joy he gives to young people, and how they grow inside.
He sees how his investment increases, and what an innovation it is for society.
He therefore gets two returns: financial and emotional.

Using money for the benefit of mankind creates positive energy.

The older generation will recognize that money only has VALUE if they make it available and provide it to other people – the young generation.
Hereby, we recall the enthusiasm that drove them as younger people.

Would you like to pass something on – by which you are remembered?

*"The highest reward for man's toil
is not what he gets for it,
but what he becomes by it."*
John Ruskin (1819-1900)

Would you want to use part of your wealth to leave something significant and valuable behind for humanity?

In my life, I have experienced people who have left behind chaos after their deaths:

- children who fought over their inheritance, while lawyers destroyed a large part of it through fees.
- heirs who squandered money by having a "good lifestyle".
- family members who drove an entrepreneur's business into bankruptcy.

I once suggested to a good friend and very wealthy businessman to build LIFE and VALUE schools worldwide using his offshore assets.

However, his EGO and thinking patterns as well as his convictions about life did not permit him to make any changes using his money – and so there was no regularization of his affairs.

I advised him to repatriate the money and make it legal. Because I advocate that people earn their money legally and pay their corresponding taxes.

After my friend passed away, the children from his first marriage started to fight with his ex-wife for the legacy of US$ 100 million. The attorneys repatriated the money. US$ 80 million had to be paid to the tax authorities. The remaining US$ 20 million were distributed among many heirs, who used it for their own needs.

Imagine the good that could be done with money, if people would not let their EGO govern them.

In the U.S., **Bill & Melinda Gates** and **Warren Buffet** have inspired affluent people to give back a part of their assets to society. But there are no set recommendations of where the money has to go. That's up to each individual.

These "Giving Pledge Members" could help change the world by donating their money to the FUND that benefits the next generation. In the end we will leave the earth, but our money will stay here.

It is our vision that money should be made available for people in society. This means that our money ought to do good for others – our families and other people.

What have our "MONEY drivers" been till today?
They have been financial returns and
finding good "deals" in order to make money.

But: Isn't HEALTH more important?
Isn't EDUCATION more important?
Isn't having a content FEELING not more important?

Will financial return also be the future MONEY driver?

Perhaps people will realize that their wealth lies in their potential.

They will exchange money for the real needs in their lives.

Money will therefore no longer have excessive importance.

Because people will have learnt to give and take MONEY with gratitude and love.

What INTENTION do you follow with your MONEY?

What VALUE does MONEY have for you?

Does it bring you JOY? Does it give you MEANING?

Does it give you a good feeling
to have money in your BANK?

Do you FEAR losing money?

Would you like to take RESPONSIBILITY
for your money?

Would you use a portion of your assets
in order to leave something VALUABLE
behind for humanity?

FUND for the next Generation

*"If you want to build a ship, don't drum up the men
to gather wood, divide the work,
and give orders. Instead, teach them
to yearn for the vast and endless sea."*

Antoine de Saint-Exupéry

The **FUND for the next Generation** invests in:
EDUCATION, HEALTH and PEOPLE.
It invests in the real economy – in people, agriculture, drinking water and new energies.
We therefore promote entrepreneurship, and create jobs.
The fund grants loans, and participates in business.

It is a Fund for the new generation – for our children and grandchildren.
Ultimately, it's about HEALTH – our own and that of people in general.
Everything is HEALTH related – whether we invest in agriculture, drinking water, new energy or education.

So we invest MONEY in people – in their capabilities and "ideas".
We support the young generation by leveraging MONEY with SPIRIT and accompanying them in their life and business.
The result is: they work with HEART and vision. They are full of energy and enthusiasm.
They create new technologies, and innovations in the field of environment and energy, communications,

health, and in the fields of medicine, education, training and child education, nutrition and housing.

These people need capital in order to implement their business ideas.
The FUND provides this capital in the shape of loans or equity investments.
At the same time, the lenders are mentors for the young entrepreneurs and pass their knowledge on to them.

The transfer has to pass a process of appraisal.
The values and framework for the transfer from the older to the younger generation is set by older and wiser people in a "Council of Elders". The Council of Elders accompanies the process of investment and provides the young people with their experience and knowledge.

The Fund:
People will leave this fund a portion of their assets, or agree that their inheritance after they pass on, will go to this fund.

Companies and banks will pay a portion of their profits into this Generation Fund.

Unclaimed and unidentified monies in banks and other institutions are also transferred to this Fund.

My own Experiences

"If one door closes, there are bigger
and better doors trying to open.
Don't get jammed in the half-closed door. Let it close.
Be ready for the new doors
that wish to open all the way for you!"
Unknown author

In the first half of my life, I managed a lot of money because I was part of the international banking industry for 30 years. So, I became aware of the irresponsible handling of money. The goal for many people was and still is to earn a very high return of their money. At the same time they are very afraid of monetary loss.

I think that our money system has served mankind very well until today. But we are now experiencing a new awareness, which requires a new system.

This is because we have realized that our present system and therefore the handling of money does not make us happy long term, and across generations.

However in the first part of my life, my awareness was not sensitized enough about the other riches in life – the immaterial richness. That, I had to learn in the second half of my life.

In order to become aware of this immaterial richness, I had to experience losing a great part of my outer richness.

I let it go very reluctantly, and desperately tried to hold onto it. So the process of release was very painful. I was devastated. All my subsequent efforts to reverse this experience and get my money back were in vain. But deep inside me I knew that this was meant to be.

I went through a major transformation. I had to learn that money is not everything on earth.
I reflected on it. I studied the biographies of people who had become very wealthy – the magnates and moguls: the Medicis, the Fuggers, Alfred Nobel, Paul Getty, the Onassis's, Agnelli's, Kennedy's, Flick's, Krupp's, Thyssen's, Quandt's and Edmond Safra.

I learnt about their relationship and their children's relationship with money. I asked myself whether these magnates used money and took care of their treasures in a worthy and benevolent way?
And I came to the conclusion that INCIDENTS in life, – like accidents, misfortune or diseases – have a connection to MONEY – how money was originally generated.

And I studied the lives of "enlighted" and wise humans. Very slowly, I came to the awareness that everything has a meaning.

Now it is my life purpose to create a link between MONEY and MEANING, and give people a deeper insight into MONEY. And I would like to contribute to making a better world for all of us.

"What lies behind us and what lies ahead of us are tiny matters compared to what lies within us."
Ralph Waldo Emerson